ENDANGERED!

DOLPHINS

Casey Horton

Series Consultant: James G. Doherty
General Curator, The Bronx Zoo, New York

BENCHMARK BOOKS

MARSHALL CAVENDISH

NEW YORK

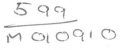

Benchmark Books
Marshall Cavendish Corporation
99 White Plains Road
Tarrytown, New York 10591-9001

©Marshall Cavendish Corporation, 1996

Library of Congress Cataloging-in-Publication Data

Horton, Casey.
    Dolphins / Casey Horton.
        p.   cm. — (Endangered!)
    Includes bibliographical references (p.   ) and index.
    Summary: Describes different kinds of dolphins, including the
bottlenose dolphin, Commerson's dolphin, and Chinese river dolphin,
and discusses how they live and what can be done to save them from
extinction.
    ISBN 0-7614-0216-0
    1. Dolphins—Juvenile literature.   2. River dolphins—Juvenile
literature.   3. Endangered species—Juvenile literature.
[1. Dolphins. 2. Endangered species.]   I. Title.   II. Series.
QL737.C432H65 1995
599.5'3—dc20   95-9100
                                                           CIP
                                                           AC

Printed in Hong Kong

PICTURE CREDITS
*The publishers would like to thank the following for supplying the photographs
used in this book:* Ardea 18, 22, 27; Bruce Coleman 24; Frank Lane Picture
Agency (FLPA) 5, 6, 9, 10, 17, 20, 21, 23; FLPA/Jeff Jacobson/Earthviews 16;
FLPA/Stephen Leatherwood/Earthviews 25; FLPA/Sunset FC, 2, 4, 8, 11, 13, 14,
29, BC; Natural History Photographic Agency 7, 26; Oxford Scientific Films 28.

Series created by Brown Packaging

Front cover: Bottlenose dolphin.
Title page: Killer whales.
Back cover: Killer whales.

Contents

Introduction

Dolphins are some of the best known and most beloved animals. They are also very intelligent and often friendly to humans. Although they look like fish and spend all their time in the water, dolphins are not fish but **mammals**. They are closely related to whales. In fact, some of the larger dolphins are called whales because of their size, even though scientists have decided they are actually dolphins!

A bottlenose dolphin poses for the camera. The bottlenose is the most familiar of all dolphins. "Flipper," the star of the TV program, was a bottlenose.

There are nearly 40 kinds of dolphins. In the past, other kinds existed, but they became **extinct** because they could not **adapt** to natural changes in the world around them. Many of today's dolphins are in danger of dying out, too. The difference is that these dolphins are not threatened by natural changes but by people's activities. For example, now that there are laws against whaling, some people are hunting dolphins instead for their meat and oil.

Dolphins are divided into marine dolphins, which live in the sea, and river dolphins. In this book, we will look at several kinds of threatened dolphins – at how they live and how they can be saved.

Though it has the word "whale" in its name, the short-finned pilot whale is in reality a big dolphin – it can be up to 20 ft (6.1 m) long.

Marine Dolphins

Most dolphins live in the sea. In fact more than 30 kinds of dolphins are marine dolphins. This group includes the most familiar of the dolphins – the bottlenose – as well as the six dolphins known as whales because of their large size.

Marine dolphins range in size from Heaviside's dolphin, which is 4 ft (1.2 m) long and weighs about 88 lb (40 kg), to the killer whale. This giant dolphin can be almost ten times as long as a Heaviside's – and 200 times as heavy.

With their graceful, streamlined bodies, marine dolphins are completely at home in the ocean. When they want to, they can flash through the water like a speeding torpedo. Or they can leap and jump and even travel along upright balanced on their tails. About the only limit on their

A pantropical spotted dolphin leaps from the water as it swims. Young dolphins leap for fun. Older dolphins also jump to warn others of danger.

activities is that they cannot breathe underwater. Every so often, dolphins must come to the surface and take a gulp of air. A dolphin's nose is on the top of its head. It is known as the blowhole and closes when the animal is underwater so that it does not get water in its lungs. It is because they cannot breathe underwater that dolphins drown when they get caught up in fishing nets.

Some kinds of marine dolphins live close to shore, some live far out at sea, while some are happy to live in either place. Some can even come and go between salt water and freshwater, and one kind – the tucuxi (pronounced too-KOO-shee) – is even more unusual. Scientists believe there are actually two separate types of tucuxi: one that lives only in salt water and another that lives only in freshwater.

A trapped tucuxi is released from a fishing net. The tucuxi lives along South America's coast and in the continent's Amazon and Orinoco rivers.

7

Marine Dolphins

Marine dolphins are unafraid of people and often swim and play with them. Sometimes they allow swimmers to grab hold of a fin and hitch a ride. Dolphins have even been known to help people who have gotten into difficulty while swimming. People who have touched a dolphin say that the animal's skin is not slippery as you would expect, but feels velvety.

Marine dolphins live in family groups, known as **schools**, or, in the case of killer whales, **pods**. The members "speak" to one another by making clicking, chirping, and whistling sounds. Marine dolphins also use sounds to find out what is in the water around them. As it swims along, a dolphin sends out a sound ahead of itself.

Marine dolphins, like the bottlenose, have two flippers, a single fin on their backs, and a tail that is flat, not upright like that of a fish.

The sound waves travel through the water until they hit an object. Then they bounce back, or echo, to the dolphin. In this way, the dolphin can tell how far away the object is. It can also tell how big it is. This skill is called **echolocation**, and is also used by river dolphins. It is similar to the sonar that warships use to find submerged submarines.

Besides echolocation, marine dolphins may have another remarkable skill. Some scientists believe that dolphins carry a sort of map of the ocean in their heads. Using this, they swim along underwater "highways" to where they want to go. Sometimes, though, it seems that marine dolphins make a wrong turn. When this happens, they may become stranded on a beach or rocky shore. Unable to get back into the water by themselves, they die unless people are there to help them.

Big dolphins, like these long-finned pilot whales, are regularly stranded along coasts. Scientists think that a group loses its way and runs ashore before it realizes its mistake.

Because marine dolphins are so eager and quick to learn, many have been captured and kept in **dolphinaria**, where they entertain the public. People cannot agree on whether this is a good thing or not. Some say that by meeting dolphins people become more interested in them and their problems. Others think that keeping dolphins in **captivity** is cruel and can harm them.

It is possible that almost all marine dolphins are at risk in the wild. They face many threats. Besides getting entangled in fishing nets and being hunted, they are harmed by ocean **pollution** and killed as pests.

A killer whale performs for a delighted crowd at Sea World in San Diego, California. The killer whale is sometimes known as the orca.

Killer Whale

The mighty killer whale is by far the biggest of the all the dolphins. Males can grow to more than 30 ft (9 m) long and can weigh over 8 tons. Females are smaller at about 23 ft (7 m) in length and over 4 tons in weight. The killer whale has a black back, with a gray patch behind the fin, a white patch behind the eye, and a white belly.

Killer whales are found in all the oceans of the world, both along coasts and far out to sea. They usually live in pods of between 4 and 40 animals. A pod usually consists of one adult male, a number of adult females, and some younger males and females.

Unlike many marine dolphins, the killer whale does not have a noticeable "beak." Instead, its whole head is rounded.

Killer Whale

Killer whales hunt in groups. They eat fish, squid, octopus, and smaller sea creatures. They also chase and kill penguins and other seabirds, as well as turtles and seals. In South America, killer whales take sea lions from the shore. The whales ride up to the beach with the surf, snatch a sea lion, and then slide back into the water with the next wave. Sometimes, killer whales hunt other dolphins, and a pod may even attack an enormous blue whale or sperm whale.

Scientists believe that the killer whale is at risk in some places. Many years ago, whaling was a big industry. People burned whale oil lamps and ate whale meat. Today this practice has pretty much stopped, but some fishermen still

Areas where the killer whale can be found

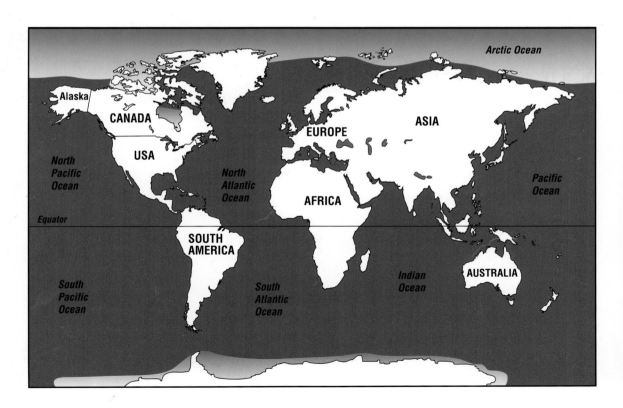

shoot killer whales. They believe they take too many fish.

Another threat is from pollution. In some areas, the sea contains large amounts of dangerous chemicals. These have been washed into the water from farmland or pumped out of factories. Fish and other marine animals take in these chemicals in their food. Killer whales then eat these animals and become poisoned. Many governments have agreed to control the amount of dangerous materials they dump in the sea. But unless these agreements are put into effect, the seas will continue to get dirtier and dirtier, and marine life will continue to suffer.

An adult killer whale and a calf leap from the water together. When it is born, a killer whale calf may be more than 8 ft (2.4 m) long.

Bottlenose dolphins usually have bluish gray backs and light gray sides. Their underparts may be light gray, whitish, or pinkish in color.

Bottlenose Dolphin

The bottlenose dolphin gets its name from its beak, which is 8 in (20 cm) long and pointed at the tip. Males can weigh up to 440 lb (200 kg) and grow to be 12 ft (3.7 m) long. The females are a little smaller.

Bottlenose dolphins can be found in parts of the world where the waters are always warm or where they are **temperate**. (In temperate waters, the temperature varies but it is never very hot or very cold.) They live mainly along coasts but are also found in smaller numbers in deep water far out to sea.

Like most other kinds of marine dolphins, bottlenose dolphins live in schools. These are made up of 10-25 males, females, and young. Bottlenose dolphins feed on small fish, such as catfish and eels, and on squid and shrimp. They can dive as deep as 1000 ft (305 m) in search of food and can stay underwater for about 15 minutes before returning to the surface to breathe.

More bottlenose dolphins have been taken into captivity than any other kind of dolphin. Some have gone to dolphinaria; others to research centers. Scientists have been criticized for using captive dolphins for research. The scientists argue that what they learn from these creatures can help them save other endangered dolphins.

Areas where the bottlenose dolphin is mainly found (red), and where it can be found in smaller numbers (brown)

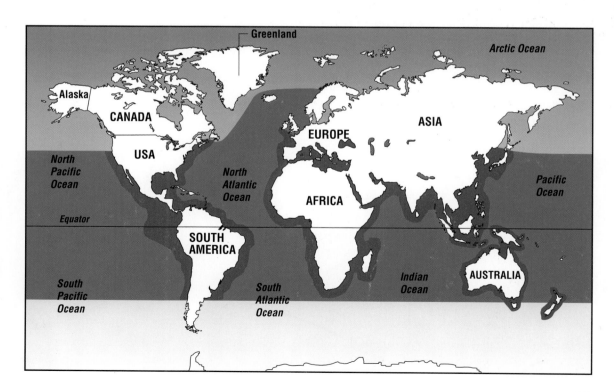

Bottlenose Dolphin

In the wild, **conservationists** are worried about the effects of fishing on the bottlenose dolphin. Many dolphins get tangled and drown in **gillnets** put out to catch fish. In some areas, bottlenose dolphins are deliberately hunted for their meat and oil. Fishermen also kill dolphins as pests.

Conservationists believe that the bottlenose dolphin is at risk. But they need more information about this dolphin in the wild before they can make a plan to save it. In the meantime, they are trying to persuade fishermen not to use gillnets. They also want laws passed to make it illegal to hunt dolphins. The laws would help, though, only if many countries obeyed them.

A bottlenose dolphin feeding on fish. When they come across a large group of fish, bottlenose dolphins often herd them together to make them easier to catch.

A group of three pantropical spotted dolphins in the Gulf of Mexico.

Pantropical Spotted Dolphin

The pantropical spotted dolphin is long and slim. Its back is generally gray in color, with lighter-colored spots; its belly is usually light, with dark spots. The amount of spots varies from dolphin to dolphin and often depends on where it lives. A spotted dolphin living near the coast often has more spots than one that lives out at sea.

This dolphin is found mainly in **tropical** waters in the Pacific, Atlantic, and Indian oceans. Males measure 6 ft 6 in-7 ft 3 in (2-2.2 m) in length and weigh about 220 lb (100 kg). Females are a little smaller than males. The largest pantropical spotted dolphins are found along coasts.

Spotted dolphins can get tangled in nets and drown. This net is not for fishing but a net put out to stop sharks from coming near a tourist beach.

Pantropical spotted dolphins swim near the surface of the ocean, sometimes in schools of several thousands, feeding on fish and squid. In some areas, when these schools approach land, fishermen come out in boats to hunt them. The fishermen follow the dolphins until they force them into a narrow bay. Trapped, the dolphins can easily be killed. Bottlenose dolphins are also caught in this way.

The biggest problem pantropical spotted dolphins face, though, is from tuna fishermen. For reasons scientists do not know, schools of yellowfin tuna often swim along with spotted dolphins. In parts of the Pacific Ocean, fishermen know that this happens. When they see spotted dolphins,

18

they encircle them in huge nets and drag them alongside the boat together with the tuna. In this way, the fishermen catch plenty of tuna, but they also capture many dolphins. Some fishermen release as many dolphins as possible from their nets. Others use nets from which dolphins can escape. Nevertheless, many dolphins drown.

Only yellowfin tuna is caught in this way. Yellowfin makes up only a tiny part of all the tuna caught in the world each year. For this small amount, millions of dolphins have died. Some large tuna canning companies have now stopped accepting tuna that is caught by netting dolphins. Others, though, are still buying it, and the number of pantropical spotted dolphins continues to fall.

Areas where the pantropical spotted dolphin can be found

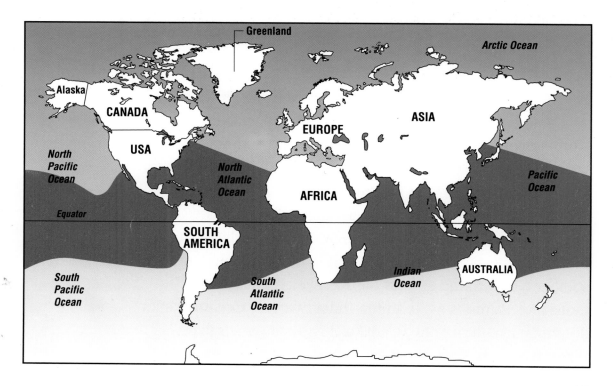

Areas where Commerson's dolphin is mainly found

Commerson's Dolphin

Commerson's dolphins are black and white and have a rounded head with no noticeable beak. They are usually 4 ft-4 ft 6 in (1.2-1.4 m) long and weigh 80-110 lb (36-50 kg). Males and females are about the same size.

Commerson's dolphins are found off the southeast coast of South America and near the Falkland Islands. In summer, some are also found around the Kerguelen Islands, thousands of miles away in the Indian Ocean. Commerson's dolphins usually live in groups of less than ten animals, feeding on fish, shrimp, and squid.

Like the much larger killer whale, Commerson's dolphin (above) has striking black-and-white markings.

The South American crab-fishing industry has put Commerson's dolphin in danger. The fishermen have trouble getting enough bait, so they kill dolphins, cut them up, and use the meat to attract crabs. Along with Commerson's, they also use Peale's dolphin and the Chilean black dolphin. There are laws against this practice, but illegal hunting still goes on. Unless this can be controlled, all these rare dolphins may disappear forever.

Commerson's dolphins ride on the wave created by a boat. Many marine dolphins like to do this.

River Dolphins

River dolphins look a little like bottlenose dolphins that have had their beaks stretched. There are only five kinds, and all but one live in the slow-moving waters of the world's great rivers. The odd one out is the La Plata dolphin, or franciscana, which is found in South American coastal waters rather than in rivers.

Unlike their marine cousins, river dolphins tend not to live in large schools, but in small groups, pairs, or even alone. Nor do they often leap out of the water or ride along

A Chinese river dolphin moves through the gloom of its Yangtze River home. River dolphins, unlike marine dolphins, have flexible necks and can move their heads from side to side.

on the waves created by boats. Except when they come to the surface to breathe, they are usually invisible in the murky water. Even in the shallows, it is often so dark that the dolphins must use their excellent echolocation skills to find food. River dolphins do not see well in any case, and the Ganges and Indus river dolphins are almost blind.

River dolphins are the most endangered of all dolphins, and all five kinds are at risk. The main reason is that people are making changes to the waterways in which the river dolphins make their homes. By building dams and draining lakes, people are leaving these shy animals with fewer and fewer places to live.

The Ganges river dolphin's front teeth are longer than its back teeth and can be seen even when the dolphin's mouth is closed.

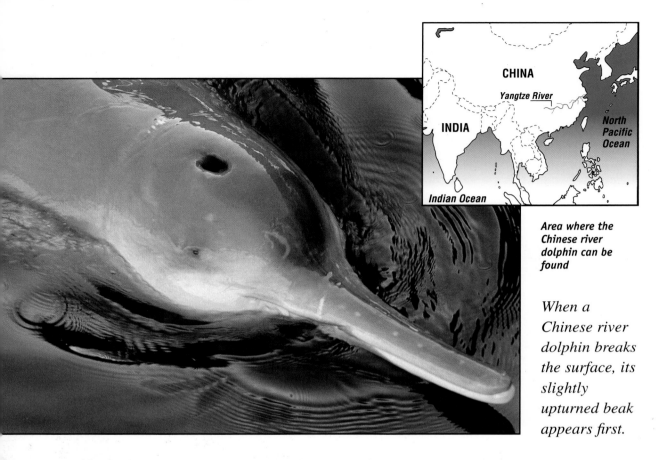

Area where the Chinese river dolphin can be found

When a Chinese river dolphin breaks the surface, its slightly upturned beak appears first.

Chinese River Dolphin

The Chinese river dolphin, or beiji, lives in China's Yangtze River and is sometimes known as the Yangtze river dolphin. It also makes its home in the smaller rivers that flow into the Yangtze and in nearby lakes. The dolphin weighs 160-265 lb (73-120 kg) and measures 5-8 ft (1.5-2.4 m) in length. Its body is blue-gray with whitish areas on the belly. Chinese river dolphins often live in pairs, but sometimes they can be found in groups of 3-12. They feed only on fish.

The Chinese river dolphin is probably the most endangered dolphin of all. Only about 200 are left in the wild. Chinese river dolphins have been accidentally caught by fishermen using rods and lines and have been run down by motor boats. They also suffer when people drain lakes to provide more land for farming.

In China, it is illegal to kill river dolphins deliberately, but they still get killed accidentally. To prevent accidental dolphin deaths, the Chinese government is trying to teach people to be more careful on the water. It also plans to set up **reserves** on the Yangtze River, where the dolphin can live in peace.

A captive Chinese river dolphin at the Institute of Marine Biology in Wuhan, China, where scientists are working on programs to save river dolphins.

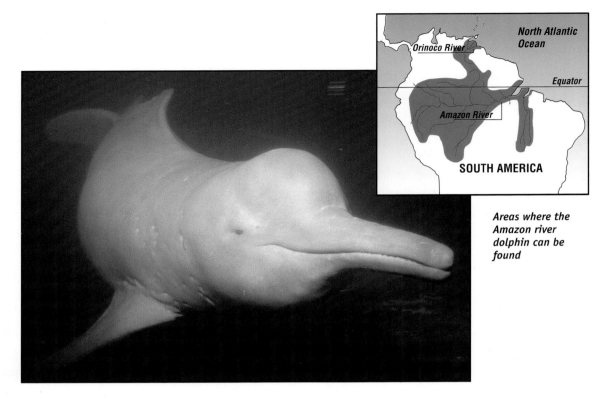

Areas where the Amazon river dolphin can be found

Amazon River Dolphin

Amazon river dolphins measure 6 ft 6 in-8 ft (2-2.4 m) in length and weigh 175-285 lb (80-130 kg). Like all river dolphins, they have a long, narrow beak that contains about 100 teeth. They look as though they are always smiling.

These dolphins usually live alone or in groups of up to 15 animals. They can be found in the Orinoco and Amazon rivers in South America. Each year, these great rivers overflow, leaving the surrounding forests and grasslands underwater for long periods. When this happens, the Amazon river dolphins move away from the main rivers and swim off into the flooded forests hunting for food.

The bulge on the Amazon river dolphin's head contains a special organ. Scientists are not sure what it does, though some think it is used in echolocation.

When the water levels start to fall again at the start of the dry season, the dolphins return to the main channels.

Amazon river dolphins feed on fish and other river creatures, including turtles. These dolphins can see better than other river dolphins. Even so, they find their food mainly by echolocation and by digging in the mud with their beaks. These have small, sensitive hairs on them that help the dolphins to feel objects in the mud.

No one is sure how many Amazon river dolphins are left, but they are in danger. People hunt them for their meat and oil. Fishermen accidentally catch them in their nets. Amazon river dolphins are powerful creatures and can sometimes tear themselves free of the nets. Usually, however, they get tangled and drown. Some South American countries have made it illegal to hunt or injure

An Amazon river dolphin swims along the surface. Like Chinese river dolphins, these animals are often hit by boats and injured or killed.

Amazon river dolphins. But it is difficult to stop the people from breaking the law.

The biggest threat to the Amazon river dolphins comes from changes people are making to the rivers. There are plans to build dams on the Amazon. If these go ahead, Amazon river dolphins – and the tucuxi, which also lives on this river – could be trapped in small areas. Apart from having limited food there, the dolphins would be separated from others of their kind. They would therefore be unable to breed. If Amazon river dolphins are to survive, river projects such as dams will need to be carefully managed.

Amazon river dolphins sometimes swim upside down when they are searching for food.

As we have seen, because dolphins live underwater, it is difficult for scientists to count and study them. Therefore, they do not know exactly how many are left. What is certain, though, is that dolphins are in danger. Hunting and fishing need to be controlled. Pollution needs to be stopped. Making these changes will be expensive and so will not be easy, especially for poor countries. However, if no action is taken, dolphins – and many other marine and river animals – may disappear forever.

Bottlenose dolphins (below) can live to be over 30 years old. Female killer whales can reach the age of 90!

Useful Addresses

For more information about dolphins and how you can help protect them, contact these organizations:

Cousteau Society
930 W. 21st Street
Norfolk, VA 23517

Dolphin Research Center
P. O. Box 522875
Marathon Shores, FL 33052

Greenpeace USA
1436 U Street NW
Washington, D.C. 20039

National Wildlife Federation
1400 16th Street NW
Washington, D.C. 20036

U.S. Fish and Wildlife Service
Endangered Species and Habitat
Conservation
400 Arlington Square
18th and C Streets NW
Washington, D.C. 20240

World Wildlife Fund
1250 24th Street NW
Washington, D.C. 20037

World Wildlife Fund Canada
90 Eglinton Avenue East
Suite 504
Toronto
Ontario M4P 2Z7

Further Reading

The Bottlenose Dolphin Virginia Schomp (New York: Dillon, 1994)

Dolphins and Porpoises Dorothy Hinshaw Patent (New York: Holiday House, 1987)

Endangered Wildlife of the World (New York: Marshall Cavendish Corporation, 1993)

Nine True Dolphin Stories Margaret Davidson (New York: Scholastic, 1990)

Project Dolphin J. Bailey (Austin, TX: Raintree Steck-Vaughn, 1994)

The Sea World Book of Dolphins Stephen Leatherwood and Randall Reeves
    (New York: Harcourt, Brace, 1987)

Whales, Dolphins and Porpoises Mark Carwardine (New York:
    Dorling Kindersley, 1992)

Wildlife of the World (New York: Marshall Cavendish Corporation, 1994)

Glossary

Adapt: To change in order to survive in new conditions.

Captivity: Confinement; for dolphins, usually in a pool.

Conservationist (Kon-ser-VAY-shun-ist): A person who protects and preserves the Earth's natural resources, such as animals, plants, and soil.

Dolphinarium (Dol-fin-AIR-eey-um – plural **dolphinaria**): A place where dolphins are kept to perform for people.

Echolocation (Ek-o-lo-KAY-shun): The skill that dolphins use to find objects underwater. The dolphin sends out a sound. The sound waves move until they strike an object. Then they bounce back, or echo, to the dolphin. When the dolphin receives this sound, it can tell how big the object is and where it is in the water.

Extinct (Ex-TINKT): No longer living anywhere in the world.

Gillnet: A fishing net made of fine thread and with small holes.

Mammal: A kind of animal that is warm-blooded and has a backbone. Most mammals are covered with fur or have hair. Females have glands that produce milk to feed their young.

Pod: The name given to a family group of killer whales.

Pollution (Puh-LOO-shun): Materials, such as garbage, fumes, and chemicals, that damage the environment.

Reserve: A place that has been set aside for plants and animals to live in without being harmed. For dolphins, this means an area of sea or a section of river.

School: The name given to a group of marine dolphins.

Temperate: Neither very hot nor very cold. For example, temperate waters.

Tropical: Having to do with or found in the tropics, the warm region of the Earth near the Equator. For example, tropical waters.

Index